AF589994

Asking
Awesome
Questions

Welcome to the exhilarating world of "The Fearless Girl and the Little Guy with Greatness!" In this third installment, we will focus on curiosity, observation, being an efficient problem solver, and asking awesome questions.

The Fearless Girl and the Little Guy with Greatness are two kids who absolutely love to explore! They are also eager to encourage their friends to do the very same. When they explore, they pay attention to all sorts of details and patterns that other children might miss. When they face a problem, they stay positive and brainstorm different ways to solve it.

One of their favorite things to do is to ask questions that earn answers beyond a simple "yes" or "no." By asking such questions, they begin to gain a better understanding of the conversation taking place.

At the end of each section of this book, there are special "Try It Activities" where — just like The Fearless Girl and the Little Guy with Greatness — you can practice becoming exceptional at asking awesome questions!

Written by

Mort Greenberg &
Carly Greenberg

This is a work of fiction. Names, characters, places and incidents either are the product of the author's imagination or are used fictitiously. Any resemblance to actual events or locales or persons, living or dead, is entirely coincidental.

Design: Heri Susanto
Illustrations: Dian Kartika Abidin

First Paperback edition June 2023

ISBN 979-8-9880534-2-2

Published by TuckEmIn
www.tuckemin.com

Introduction

Tuck Em' In Publishing is a father and daughter effort that creates and publishes books for kids. Our mission is to Motivate and Inspire. Our vision is to help kids make the most of their todays and tomorrows.

The Fearless Girl and The Little Guy with Greatness is a book series that aims to share the following message: anything is possible for any kid if they put their mind to it.

Kids, you can find in our books ways to handle yourselves in important, real-life situations. Caregivers, you will find ways to push the kids in your life to be their best selves. Through our books, we hope to encourage families to communicate more effectively with each other.

"Asking Awesome Questions" is the third installment in The Fearless Girl and The Little Guy with Greatness series. This book will map out five skills: (1) Curiosity, (2) Observational Skills, (3) Problem-Solving, (4) The Art of Asking Questions, and (5) Logic and Reasoning — all of which are crucial for critical thinking.

Mort Greenberg and his daughter, **Carly Greenberg**, have embarked on numerous adventures together across the mountains of the United States. They also built self-guided, 18-hour day races in London, Paris, Milan, Venice, Murano, Burano, Rome, Buenos Aires, Tigre, Montevideo, Valparaiso, Santiago, Asuncion, and more.

This father and daughter team has worked through and overcome the same situations that you, as a parent, are experiencing now with a young daughter or son. Each skill in the book was inspired by an actual conversation that took place over the years from when Carly was five to ten years old.

You Can Follow Mort and Carly on social media:

@mortgreenberg

@greenbergcarly

@mortgreenberg

@carlygreenberg

This Book Belongs to

____

Today's Date : ______________________________

Sections (Table Of Contents)

"By honing these key topics, you and your friends will establish solid critical thinking and questioning skills, which are guaranteed to serve you well throughout your entire lives."

The Power of Curiosity

Have you ever wondered how things work or why things happen? Do you like asking questions and learning about new things? If you answered yes to any of the above questions, then congratulations! You have a quality that's exceedingly special: **curiosity!**

Curiosity means to be interested in something and want to know more about it. When you're curious, you're not afraid to ask questions or experiment with new things.

Let's go over some examples of curiosity. Have you ever seen a bug and wondered what kind it is? Or asked your parents how a car works? These are both great examples of being curious. Curiosity helps you to learn, explore, and discover new things, often leading to boundless exciting adventures!

Now, let's talk about some ways you can practice being curious:

Try It Activity

Ask What and Why

The first step to being curious is actively asking questions. Ask about everything! Ask about things that you see, hear, smell, and experience. For example, if you're walking outside and see a bird, you can ask, "What kind of bird is that?" or "Why is it flying in that direction?" By asking what and why questions, you are sure to learn more about the world around you.

Try It Activity

Seek Hidden Connections

Keep an eye out for similarities and differences. Compare and contrast various objects, people, or situations in order to identify patterns. To do this, you must ask yourself questions such as "What do these things have in common?" or "What sets them apart?"

Try It Activity

Be Experimental

Finally, being curious means being willing to try out new things. It can be something small, like tasting a new food, or something bigger, like engaging in a new hobby. Experimenting with new things will help you grow and discover new interests.

”

Curiosity is a powerful tool”

By constantly asking questions, exploring your surroundings, and trying out new things, you can develop your curiosity. So, keep asking questions. Who knows what crazy and exciting secrets you'll uncover!

The Importance of Observational Skills

Have you ever seen something that others didn't? Maybe you saw a bird in a tree that no one else noticed? Or how about a detail in a picture that others glossed over? If you have, then you already have excellent observational skills!

To be observant means to pay attention to details and build an awareness of your surroundings. When you have good observational skills, you pick up on things that others might miss or disregard. This is a fantastic skill to have, for it can help you learn, solve problems, and even stay safe.

Now, let's talk about some ways you can practice having the best observational skills:

Try It Activity

Pay Attention

The first step to building good observational skills is to always pay attention to your surroundings. Take notice of even the smallest of details around you, such as the color, shape, and texture of objects. For example, if you're walking in a park, make note of the different types of plants and animals around you. Take a closer look and dare to see if you can name them.

Try It Activity

Practice Memory Games

Memory games are an entertaining way of exercising your observational skills. Try playing games like "I Spy" or "Memory Match." These games require you to remember details and heighten your awareness . The more you practice, the better you'll become at noticing details — both big and small!

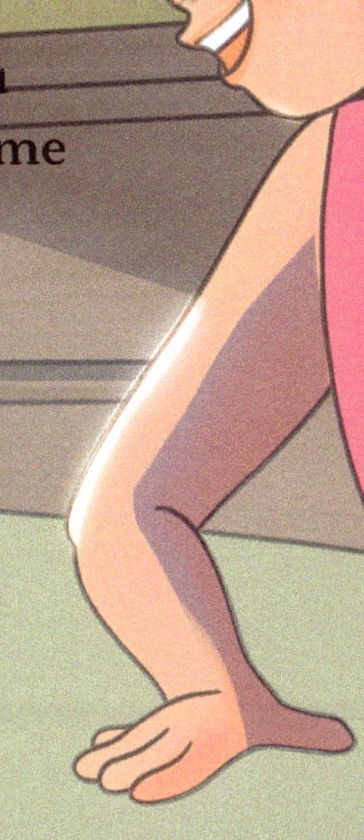

Use Your Senses

Refining your senses is a great tactic for improving your observational skills. Try closing your eyes and listening to the sounds around you. Can you hear birds chirping or leaves rustling in the wind? Try putting on a blindfold and smelling different foods. Can you guess the foods based on smell alone, or do you need to take a bite?

”

The best adventurers never stop seeking out answers for the unknown!”

By paying attention, practicing memory games, and utilizing your senses, you can improve your observational skills. So, be on the lookout. The best adventurers never stop seeking out answers for the unknown!

The Power of Problem-Solving

Have you ever faced a challenge but didn't know what to do? Maybe you couldn't locate a toy you lost, or you had trouble figuring out a math problem. When confronted with challenges such as these, you need to use our problem-solving skills in order to find a solution!

To solve a problem means to find a solution to certain obstacles you face. It is an important skill to have so that you may overcome difficulties and achieve your goals. Let's think about some examples of problem solving. Have you ever had a puzzle that you needed to solve? Or tried to build something with blocks or put a large puzzle together? These are both staple examples of problem solving. By exercising your problem-solving skills, you maximize your ability to think creatively and make decisions on the fly, therefore leading to fast and efficient solutions!

Now, let's talk about some ways you can practice problem-solving:

Try It Activity

Break The Problem Into Smaller Parts

The first step to problem-solving is breaking the problem into smaller parts. For example, if you're trying to locate a toy — rather than scrambling from one end of the house to the other — do a thorough search of each individual room. By breaking the problem into smaller parts, it becomes much more manageable and thus, easier to solve.

Try It Activity

Brainstorm Solutions

The next step to problem-solving is brainstorming solutions. This means to compiling a list of ideas for solving the problem. For instance, if you're trying to locate a lost phone or tablet, you could brainstorm solutions like asking someone for help, looking under the furniture, or retracing your steps. Brainstorming helps you expand your way of thinking so that you can invent creative solutions to all kinds of situations. It's the ultimate superpower!

Try It Activity

Take Action

The final step to problem-solving is taking action. This means to put the solutions you came up with to the test and see which one works best. If you're trying to find a lost toy, try retracing your steps first. If that doesn't work, then ask someone for help. Don't feel discouraged if one idea doesn't turn out well. Keep going at it! You will always learn from your mistakes. Think of each failure as a stepping stone towards success.

”

Keep practicing, and you’ll be amazed with how many trials you conquer”

By breaking the problem into smaller parts, brainstorming solutions, and taking action, you will become better at problem-solving. Keep practicing, and you'll be amazed with how many trials you conquer. Who knows? You might find yourself acting as the next great investigator of your time.

The Art of Asking Questions

Have you ever asked a question but only received a simple yes or no answer? But really you wanted more of an answer than yes or no. What about a question you asked where the answer you received back was not helpful to you?

When you ask questions you want to do so in a way that you are encouraging others to think about their own knowledge and experiences. This way you always get the best answers back.

Using "Who", "What", "When", "Where", "Why" and "How" in your questions makes it easier to receive great information back. Check out some of these combinations: **Who:** Who is someone you admire and why? **What:** What is something you would like to learn and how would you go about learning it? **When:** When do you like to read and what are your favorite types of books? **Where:** Where is a place you've always wanted to visit and how would you get there? **Why:** Why do you think it's important to be kind to others and who are some people that are kind to you? **How:** How can I eat healthy and what are the best foods to eat?

Now, let's talk about some ways you can practice asking great questions:

Ask Open-Ended Questions

The first step in the art of asking questions is to ask open-ended questions. This means asking questions that require more than a simple yes or no answer. In other words, they are questions that can be answered in a variety of ways based on the person you're asking. For example, you could ask, "What was your favorite part of going to the park?" rather than "Did you have fun at the park?" Open-ended questions encourage more thought-provoking and informative answers.

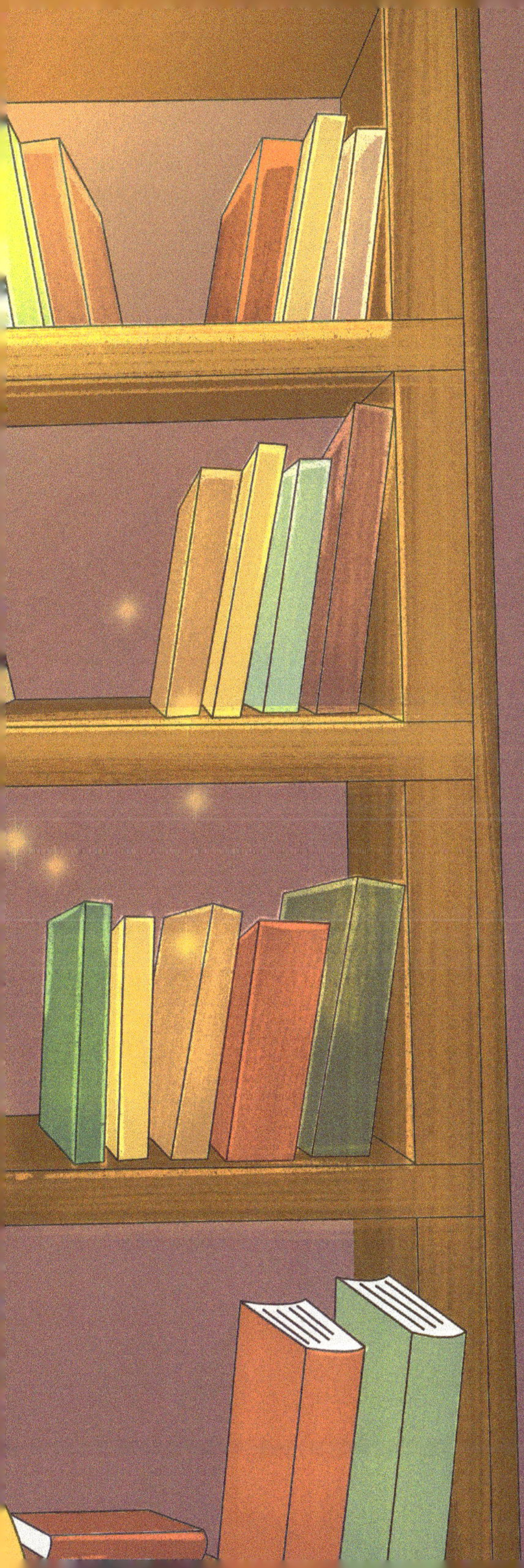

Active Listening

The next step in the art of asking questions is to use the skill of active listening. By paying attention to the person who's answering your question you will be able to best understand what they are saying and even be able to ask follow-up questions. For example, if your friend is telling you about their favorite book, you could ask, "What was your favorite part of the book?" or "Why did you like the book so much?" Active listening will help you absorb information better, and help you to ask follow up questions to get the most from all of your conversations.

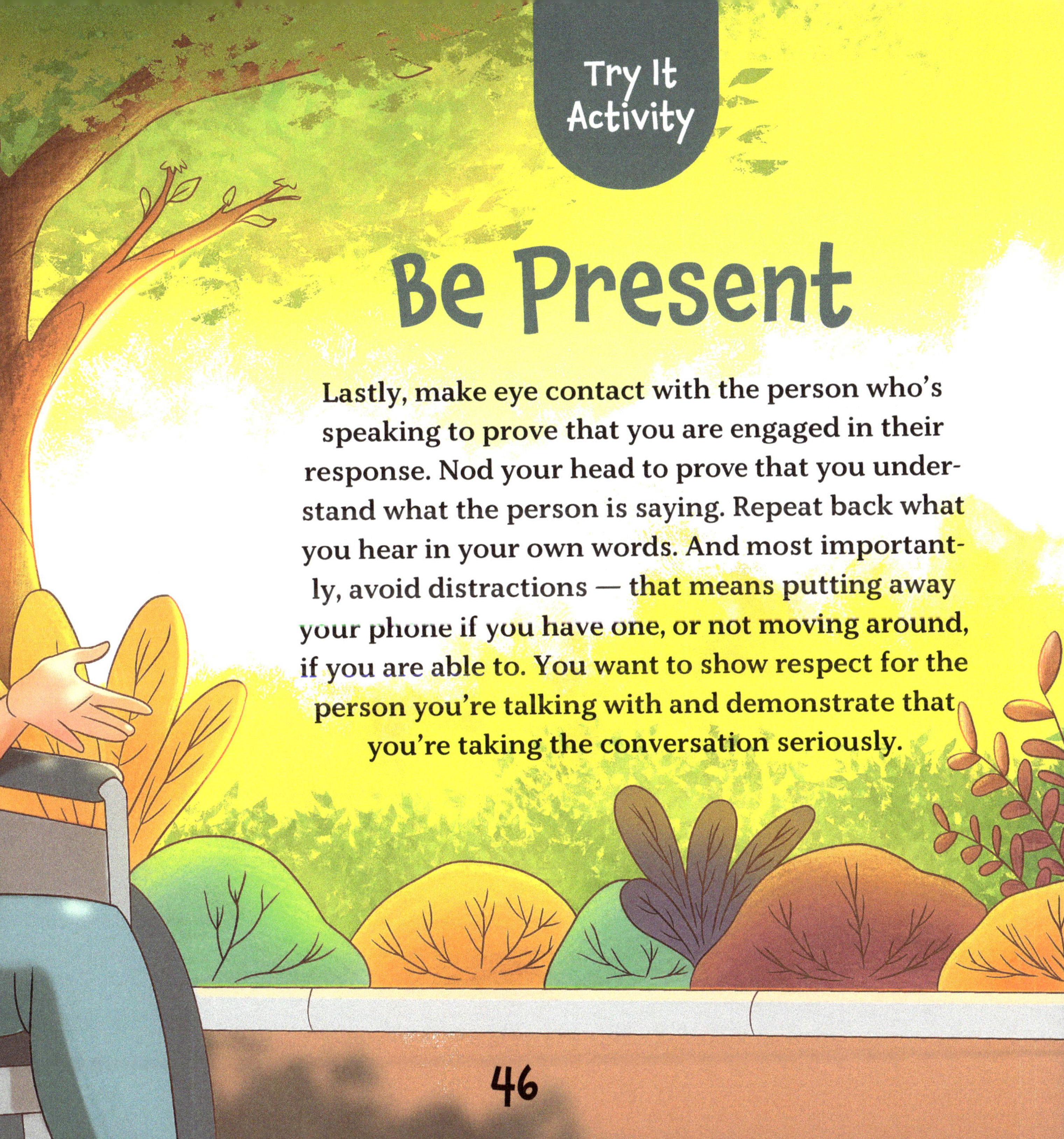

Be Present

Lastly, make eye contact with the person who's speaking to prove that you are engaged in their response. Nod your head to prove that you understand what the person is saying. Repeat back what you hear in your own words. And most importantly, avoid distractions — that means putting away your phone if you have one, or not moving around, if you are able to. You want to show respect for the person you're talking with and demonstrate that you're taking the conversation seriously.

”

Keep on working to improve the art of asking questions”

By asking open-ended questions, practicing active listening, and showing curiosity, you're opening yourself up to a whole new world of revelations. So, keep on working to improve the art of asking questions, everyone around you will appreciate how you interact with them.

The Power of Logic And Reasoning

Have you ever had to figure out how to resolve a troubling issue or make an important decision? If you have, then you've already started tapping into the power that is logic and reasoning.

Logic and reasoning are important skills to use if you want to make sense of information, solve problems, and make good decisions.

Logic is all about thinking in a systematic and organized way. It helps you make connections between different pieces of information and understand cause-and-effect relationships. Reasoning is all about using logic and evidence to make informed decisions.

Let's think about some examples of logic and reasoning. Have you ever played a game of Chess or Checkers? These games require you to plan ahead to win. Planning out your next steps forces you to apply reasoning and logic in your head before you make your next move.

Now, let's talk about some ways you can practice using logic and reasoning:

Try It Activity

Look For Patterns

The first step to using logic and reasoning is to look for patterns. Patterns are connections between different pieces of information. For example, if you're playing a game of Tic Tac Toe, you might notice that you need three in a row to win. Looking for patterns helps you think systematically and understand how things work.

Try It Activity

Make Predictions

The next step to using logic and reasoning is to make predictions. This means using what you know to make an educated guess about what might happen next. For example, if you're playing a game of connecting lines you might predict where your opponent will place their next piece based on their previous moves. Making predictions helps you plan ahead and think logically.

Try It Activity

Evaluate Evidence

Finally, evaluating evidence is an important part of using logic and reasoning. This means looking at the information available and using it to make a decision. For example, if you're trying to decide which toy to buy, you might evaluate the different features and prices to make your decision. Evaluating evidence helps you make informed decisions based on logic and reasoning.

SALE

”

Look for Patterns”

By looking for patterns, making predictions, and evaluating evidence, you can become better at using logic and reasoning to solve problems and make good decisions. So, keep practicing and who knows what exciting challenges you'll overcome next!

Conclusion

Wow! You've learned so much about curiosity, observation, problem solving, the art of asking questions, and logic and reasoning! Remember, when you're exploring the world around you, pay special attention to the details and patterns you see.

Always improving the questions that you ask is a great way to learn and become a phenomenal thinker. Always push yourself to ask questions that give you more than a "yes" or "no" answer from the person that you are talking with. Use your brain to connect pieces of information together and think about a follow up question that you can ask after your first question.

And when you're facing a problem, don't give up! Stay positive. Staying positive will help you to stay calm and figure out a solution to the problem that you are working through. If there is ever just one rule, it is "Do Not Quit!" Create positive self talk in your brain. Tell yourself that there is always another route to follow and that you just need to keep on trying. **Always keep trying! Never give up!**

Check Out

Book 4

Think to Win

About The Authors

For the past 25 years **Mort Greenberg** has been a salesperson and sales manager for technology start-ups and larger media companies. Fighting his way up from an Account Executive to a role as a division President you can guess there were many challenges that needed to be overcome. Along the way Mort launched two companies, FitAd and MindFlight and learned many hard-fought lessons that start-ups are not always successful. He is a graduate of the State University of New York at New Paltz where he studied International Relations and Economics. While in college he started a company selling screen printing and promotional items to local businesses and on-campus organizations. At the same time, he also volunteered as a Congressional District Intern for the U.S. House of Representatives. He is an Eagle Scout and in junior high school bought several newspaper routes from neighborhood kids to create his first business. Mort is also the author of the *Revenue Vs. Sales*, a three book series that you can find on Amazon.com.

Carly Greenberg attends the University of Maryland's Smith School of Business with a double major in marketing and management. Carly's twin brother has autism, and she has helped him find his voice through her unique interactions with him. He is the original little guy with greatness. Carly is the original fearless girl, always helping others, volunteering, and finding ways to do more with less - all while having to put up with a crazy dad. Carly also holds a black belt in Tae Kwon Do.

www.ingramcontent.com/pod-product-compliance
Ingram Content Group UK Ltd.
Pitfield, Milton Keynes, MK11 3LW, UK
UKHW061950290726
14090UKWH00021B/1170